MADRAS GOVERNMENT MUSEUM

Bulletin, Vol. V. No. 2.

ANTHROPOLOGY

MADRAS GOVERNMENT MUSEUM

Bulletin, Vol. V. No. 2.

ANTHROPOLOGY

THE PARAIYAN, AND THE LEGEND OF NANDAN,

REV. A. C. CLAYTON

SOME AGRICULTURAL CEREMONIES IN MALABAR

C. KARUNAKARA MENON

WITH FOUR PLATES

GYAN

Published by

GYAN

Gyan Publishing House
5, Ansari Road
Daryaganj, New Delhi-110002
Phone: 011-47034999, 9811692060
E-mail: books@gyanbooks.com

Distribution Network
gyanbooks.com
India, USA, Canada, UK, Australia, France

ISBN : 978-81-212-3875-5 (PB)
First Published, Madras, 1906

2nd Impression 2020

Printed at: Gyan Press, Delhi.

MADRAS GOVERNMENT MUSEUM.

Bulletin, Vol. V, No. 2.

ANTHROPOLOGY.

THE PARAIYAN, AND THE LEGEND OF NANDAN, BY THE REV. A. C. CLAYTON; SOME AGRICULTURAL CEREMONIES IN MALABAR, BY C. KARUNAKARA MENON.

With Four Plates.

MADRAS:
PRINTED BY THE SUPERINTENDENT, GOVERNMENT PRESS.

1906.

THE PARAIYAN.

CONTENTS.

THE PARAIYAN.

BY THE REV. A. C. CLAYTON,

Wesleyan Missionary.

---

1. It is the aim of this essay to put in order some facts about the Paraiyans, which I have learned in almost daily intercourse with them since 1892. If the meagreness of these notes is criticised, I can only plead that, so far as I know, this is the first attempt to give a general account of this people, and that it has been very difficult to gather any but partial information from them or about them.

I am indebted to many missionaries and missionary workers for occasional information, and also to the following books :—

Baines : General Report on the Census of India, 1891.
Francis : Report on the Census of India, 1901 (Madras Presidency).
Jensen : Tamil Proverbs.
Oppert : On the Original Inhabitants of Bharatavarsa.
Padfield : The Hindu at Home.
Stuart : Report on the Census of India, 1891 (Madras Presidency)

For the statements enclosed in square brackets I am indebted to Mr. K. Rangachari of the Madras Museum.

2. *Plan.*—The general outline of this paper is the same as that of the series of questions prepared by Mr. Thurston in connection with the Ethnographic Survey of the Madras Presidency, part of the Ethnographic Survey of India. The table of contents will show the more important headings, under which the facts given are arranged. The index will enable readers to find such matters as are not clearly indicated by the headings of the sections.

3. *The name Paraiyan.*—The anglicised term 'Pariah' is ordinarily applied to all the lowest classes of field-labourers, and indeed to most day labourers in the Madras Presidency. Leather-workers, cobblers, weavers of grass-mats, the hunting castes, and all the miscellaneous folk who are neither Musalmāns, nor included in the regular social

system of Hinduism, are often carelessly referred to by this name. But Hindus do not speak in this indiscriminate fashion; by 'Pariah' they mean only the special Dravidian tribes called, in Tamil, *Paraiyan* (பறையன்) and, in Telugu, *Māla* (మాల). To avoid any confusion, the word '*Paraiyan*' will be used throughout this paper, to designate the Tamil section of the 'Pariah' class that calls itself, and is called in Tamil, *Paraiyan*; and my statements will refer to them only. The late Dr. Caldwell, an acknowledged authority on all subjects connected with Tamil antiquities, derived the name Paraiyan from the Tamil word *parai* (பறை) a drum, as certain Paraiyans act as drummers at funerals, marriages, village festivals, and on all occasions when government or communal announcements are proclaimed. (Census of India Report, 1891, vol. xiii, p. 244.) Mr. H. A. Stuart, in his Report on the Madras Census of 1891, seems to question this derivation, remarking that it seems in the highest degree improbable that a large community should owe its name to an occasional occupation; adding that the word *Paraiyan* is not found in an ancient Tamil vocabulary, the *Divākaram* which dates from the eleventh century of the Christian Era, whilst the word *Pulayan*, now used in Malayālam, the language of Travancore, was then used to denote those who are now called Paraiyans. (*Ibid.*, p. 244.) Some confirmation of this is found in the legend of the Saivite saint Nandan. He is called a Pulayan in the prose version of the *Periya Purānam*, though a native of the Sholamandalam (சோழமண்டலம்), which was a distinctly Tamil kingdom. But, on the other hand, an inscription mentioned by Mr. Francis in the Census Report for 1901 shows that Paraiyans were known as Paraiyans in the eleventh century A.D. (see section 10).

Dr. Gustav Oppert (Original Inhabitants of Bharatavarsa) contends that the names of many Dravidian tribes come from two Dravidian roots, *mal* and *ku*, both meaning mountain; and that the names of the Telugu *Mālas*, of the Tamil *Malayālis* (of the west coast and of the Shevaroy hills), of the Tamil *Maravans*, and, by a very bold phonetic equation, of the Tamil *Pallans*, *Pallis*, *Paraiyans*, all mean 'the men of the hill-country' or 'the men from the hill-country.' Even the word *Valluvan* is treated in the same way. This derivation has received some attention, and is certainly not without some probability. But it is not clear to me that Dr. Oppert's equation is justifiable; and even if it is admitted, it is not obvious what it indicates, for most of the tribes referred to are not connected with the hills, do not make pilgrimages to the hill-country, or worship in the temples of the modern hill-tribes.

It is of course conceivable that the Paraiyans, and the other very distinct tribes in the list discussed by Dr. Oppert, may have been originally mountaineers, but, at present, the conjecture cannot be regarded as even a working hypothesis. While there can be no doubt of the antiquity of the Paraiyans—as I shall show in section 10 —I am driven to confess that their origin is one of the unsolved problems of Dravidian ethnology; and that their name gives no practical guidance in the matter.

The following very interesting extract from Sonnerat's Voyages is supplied by Mr. Thurston. It will be noted that this account is a hundred and twenty years old:—

Pariahs. "They are prohibited from drawing water from the wells of other castes: but have particular wells of their own near their habitations, round which they place the bones of animals that they may be known and avoided. When an Indian of any other cast permits a Paria to speak to him, this unfortunate being is obliged to hold his hand before his mouth, lest the Indian may be contaminated with his breath; and, if he is met on the highway, he must turn on one side to let the other pass. If any Indian whatever, even a Choutre, by accident touches a Paria, he is obliged to purify himself in a bath. The Brahmins cannot behold them, and they are obliged to fly when they appear . . .

Great care is taken not to eat anything dressed by a Paria, nor even to drink out of the vessel he has used; they dare not enter the house of an Indian of another caste; or, if they are employed in any work, a door is purposely made for them; but they must work with their eyes on the ground; for if it is perceived they have glanced at the kitchen, all the utensils must be broke. . . . . The infamacy of the Parias is reflected on the Europeans: last are held in more detestation, because, setting aside the little respect they have for the cow, whose flesh they eat, the Indians reproach them with spitting in their houses, and even their temples: that when drinking they put the cup to their lips, and their fingers to their mouths in such a manner that they are defiled with the spittle.* "

* Sonnerat: 'Voyage to the East Indies,' 1774 and 1781.

4. *Numbers.*—According to the Census of 1891 there were 2,059,466 persons of the Paraiyan caste in the Madras Presidency. According to the Census of 1901, the total number of Paraiyans amounted to 2,152,840. Of these 1,048,274 were males, and 1,104,566 were females. The number of Valluvans was 54,760.

5. *Distribution.*—Paraiyans are to be found throughout the Tamil districts from North Arcot to Tinnevelly, and in the southern extremity of the Native State of Travancore. In the districts of the Madras Presidency to the north of Madras and North Arcot, and in the Nizam's Dominions, Telugu Mālas take the place of the Paraiyans. The following table gives the numbers of Paraiyans according to sex in the districts where they are most numerous. The figures are taken from the Census Report of 1901.

District.	Males.	Females.	Total.
Madras	30,877	31,827	62,704
Chingleput	162,556	158,770	321,326
North Arcot	94,450	98,193	192,643
Salem	90,092	94,355	184,947
South Arcot	273,287	282,962	556,249
Tanjore	146,407	163,984	310,391
Trichinopoly	65,543	70,234	135,777
Madura	66,937	73,147	140,084
Tinnevelly	48,372	55,058	103,430

6. *Language.*—Though the Paraiyan speaks Tamil with many vulgarisms and abbreviations of inflexional suffixes, and is often exceedingly slovenly in his articulation, I have not found that his speech differs materially from ordinary Tamil. Local variants from more usual terms may occur, or some particular agricultural term may be used to the exclusion of other synonyms, and of course the use of ச for ஐ, and of ல for ழ, which distinguishes the Tamil of the southern districts from that of the districts near Madras, holds good for Paraiya Tamil as well as Vellāla Tamil. But I know no reason to distinguish between the Tamil of the Paraiyan and that of the other Tamil speaking castes. Paraiya Tamil is Tamil, in spite of the saying பறப்பேச்சு அரைப்பேச்சு, *parappēcchu araippēcchu*, "Paraiya speech is but half-speech."

Plate X.

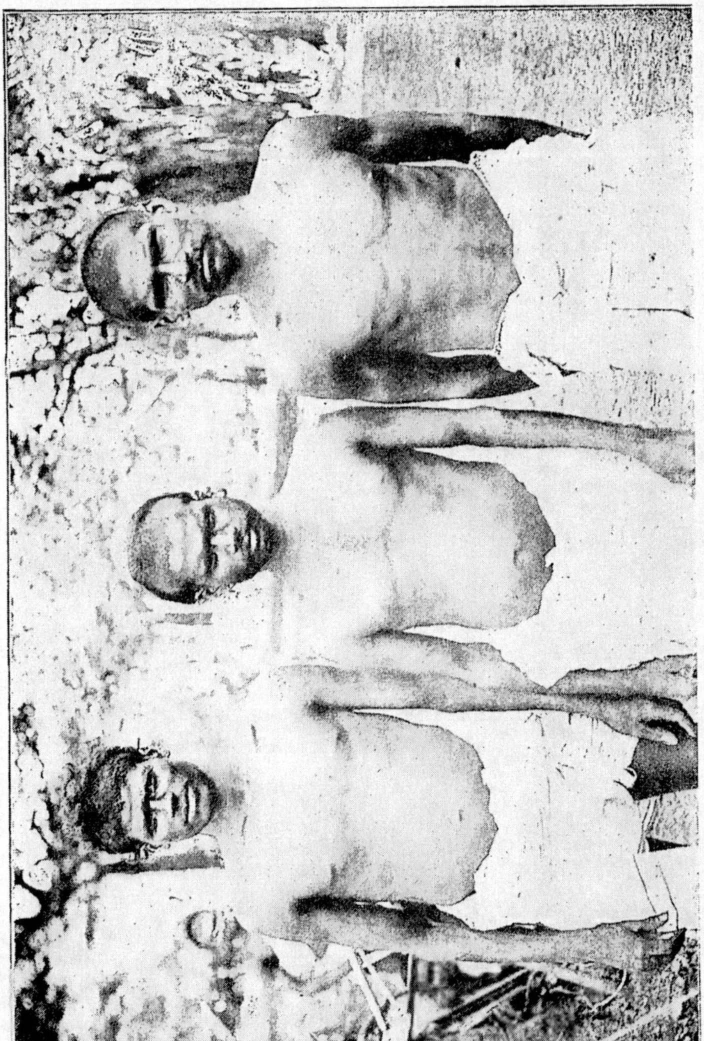

TANGALÁN PARAIYANS.

7. *Literacy.*—The number of Paraiyans who can read and write is extremely small. In 1891 the percentage of illiterates was for the whole caste 98·54. Among males the illiterates amounted to 97·25, and among females to 99·84. According to the more careful enumeration of 1901, the illiterates are 99·5 of the Paraiyan population. Among males, 99 out of one hundred persons can neither read nor write. Among females, not one in a hundred has even the rudiments of knowledge. I have no hesitation in endorsing the accuracy of the later figures.

Very few Paraiyan children attend school, and of those who do only a small proportion attend regularly.

On the other hand, it must be remembered that a very large number of Native Christians are by race Pariahs, though they now avoid the designation. Had it been possible to include them in the statistics of literacy, there can be little doubt that the percentage of illiterates would have been lowered.

8. *Names and nick-names.*—It would be very difficult to prepare a list of the names common among Paraiyans, for they have an inexhaustible stock from which to draw. Some of the most common names of males are :—

Kanni or Kanniyappan.	Subban.
Rāman or Rāmaswāmi.	Nondi.
Rāju.	Tambiran.
Vēlu.	Perumāl.
Muttan.	Vīran.
Māri.	Sellan.
Kanagan.	Amāvāsi.

In one village where the Paraiyans were almost all Vaishnavas, by profession *not* by practice, the people were all named after the multitudinous heroes of the Mahābhārata, and dirty naked Paraiya children answered to the names of Ikshvākan, Karnan, Bhiman and Draupadi!

The regular names of Tamil women are not distinctive of their caste. Tai, Pārpathi, Ammai, Kanni, Muttammāl, Rajammāl, Ammani, Selli, Gangammāl are among the most common.

It is usual to give the father's name when distinguishing one Paraiyan from another, *e.g.*, Tamburan, son of Kannan. There is no termination, prefix or agnomen to mark the Paraiyan caste. In legal documents the prefix *para* (பற) denotes the Paraiyan, *e.g.*, *Para Kanni* the Paraiyan Kanni, but this is a purely clerical formula.

The Paraiyan delights in nick-names. I have somtimes found men who had grown so accustomed to their nick-names that they had almost forgotten their less striking personal names. The following are very common :—

Nondi, lame man or woman.
Kallan, thief.
Kullan, dwarf.
Vellei, white, light complexioned.
Kannan, man " with eyes."
Muthali, crocodile.
Kudiyan, drunkard.

No special practice is observed in giving names to children; except, of course, no name is given declaring virtue or merit, lest the wrath of malevolent spirits should be aroused. The name given soon after birth is retained through life, and is used for all purposes; no second or secret name being given and reserved for religious or ceremonial purposes.

9. *Sub-divisions.*—I am not aware that among Paraiyans there are any exogamous sub-divisions, *i.e.*, sub-divisions in which the males must seek their wives from other sub-divisions. There are said to be some endogamous sub-divisions, *i.e.*, sub-divisions in which the males must marry females of the same sub-division to which they themselves belong. Valluvans are said only to marry Valluva women, and washermen are said to marry girls of their own Paraiya washerman caste. It is doubtful whether either Valluvans or washermen are very particular in the observation of this custom. Tangalān Paraiyans do not marry outside their own section, nor do the Sozhia Paraiyans. [All sections interdine.]

There are many other sub-divisions among Paraiyans. The Census of 1891 enumerates 348. Among these the chief were Tangalān (to which many domestics belong) Valangamattu, Katti, Sāmbān, Sozhia Tamil, Kongan, Koleiga, Amma, Kottai, Morasu, Kizhakkatti, Pucchai. The Konga Paraiyans beat the drums (*mēlam*) at festivals. In the Coimbatore district the Sozhia Paraiyans are said to be lowest of all. The term *Sāmbān* seems to me not to be the name of a sub-division, but rather a term of respectability equivalent to *Panakkāran* or *Muppan*. At least it is commonly used in this sense in the Coimbatore district. The report of the Census of 1901 more cautiously states that the sub-divisions are numerous. The vast majority are nominal. A few may be due to differences in occupation. (See section 37.) How slight they are is evident from the fact that they do not prevent marriage between members of different sections.

It should be noted that, while some Paraiyans eat carrion, many do not. Those who do are regarded with much contempt by those who do. (See section 38.)

10. *Antiquity.*—In the section discussing the name of the Paraiya caste, the uncertainty of any inference as to the original habitat of the Paraiyan was pointed out. I know of no legend or popular belief among these people, indicating that they think themselves to have come from any other part of the country than that where they now find themselves. There is, however, some evidence that the race has had a long past, and one in which they had independence and possibly great importance in the Peninsula.

(1) Mr. H. A. Stuart, in the Census Report for 1891, mentions that the Valluvans were priests to the Pallava Kings, before the introduction of the Brāhmans, and even for some time after it. He quotes "an unpublished Vatteluttu inscription, believed to be of the 9th century" in which the following sentence occurs:—

இத்தளி உவச்சன் ஸ்ரீவல்லுவம் பூவணவன் நியதம் ஆறுளிட்டு உவச்சப் பணிசெய்பவன்.

This may be translated—

"Sri Valluvam Puvanavan, the Uvacchan (or temple-ministrant) will employ six men daily, and do the temple service."

The inference is that the Valluvan was a man of recognised priestly rank, and of great influence. The prefix ஸ்ரீ (sri) is a notable honorific. (For the meaning of Valluvan see section 30.)

(2) By itself the above inscription would prove little, but the whole legendary history of the greatest of all Tamil poets, and one of the greatest didactic poets in the world, Tiruvalluvar, "The Holy Valluvan," confirms all that can be deduced from it. His date can only be fixed approximately, but it is probable that he flourished not later than the tenth century A.D. It is safe to say that this extraordinary sage could not have attained the fame he did, or

have received the honours that were bestowed upon him, had not the Valluvans, and therefore the Paraiyans, been in the circle of respectable society in his day. This conjecture is strengthened by the legend that he married a Vellāla girl.

The same hypothesis is the only one that will account for the education, and the vogue of the sister of the poet, the aphoristic poetess Avvei.

(3) In the Census Report, 1901, Mr. Francis mentions an inscription of the Chola King Rājarāja, dated about the eleventh century A.D., in which the Paraiyan caste is called by its own name. It had then two sub-divisions, the *nesavu* or weavers, and the *uḷavu* (உழவு) or ploughmen. The caste had even then its own hamlets, wells, and burning grounds.

There are certain privileges possessed by Paraiyans, which they could never have gained for themselves from orthodox Hinduism. These seem to be survivals of a past, in which Paraiyans held a much higher position than they do now; or at any rate show that they are as ancient in the land as any other Dravidians (Mudaliars, Pillais, &c.) whom the Paraiyan calls 'Tamils' (தமிழர்), a name which he does not apply to himself. It has been impossible to do more than gather a few of these; but those mentioned are typical.

An extract from the *Indian Antiquary*, vol. iii, p. 191, quoted in the *Madras Census Report*, 1891, mentions that at Mēlkotta and in the Aiyangar Vaishnava temple at Bailur, the Holeyars or Kanarese Paraiyans have the right of entering the temple three days in the year, specially set apart for them; and that in the great Saiva festival at Tiruvālūr in the Tanjore district, the headman of the Paraiyans is mounted on the elephant with the god, and carries his chowri (or yak-tail fly fan).

At Srīperumbudūr in the Chingleput district the Paraiyans enjoy a similar privilege, for having sheltered an image of the locally worshipped incarnation of Vishnu during a Musalmān raid.

To this day a Paraiyan annually becomes husband of Egattāl, the tutelary deity of the Black Town in Madras, and actually ties the *tāli* or marriage-token round the neck of the image.

Paraiyans are allowed to take part in pulling the cars of the idols in the great festivals at Conjeeveram, Kumbakōnam and Srīvilliputtūr. Their touch is not reckoned to defile the ropes used, so that other Hindus will also pull with them. With this may be compared the fact that the Telugu Mālas are custodians of the goddess Gauri, the bull Nandi and Ganēsa, the chief gods of the Saiva Kāpus and Balijas. It may also be noted that Kōmati Chettis, who claim to be Vaisyas, are bound to invite Mādigas to their marriages, though they take care that the latter do not hear the invitation.

Another fact which points to the ancient position of the Paraiyan in the land is the universally admitted fact that he is more intimate, so to speak, with local gods, goddesses, demons and the like, than the high caste man is or can be. I have heard well authenticated instances of Brāhman women worshipping at Paraiya shrines in order to procure children. Near Palāppattūr, in the Chingleput district, I once saw a Paraiya exorciser treating a Brāhman by uttering *mantrams* (consecrated formulæ) and waving a sickle up and down the sufferer's back, as he stood in a threshing floor.

To this may be added the very general belief that the Paraiyans know the village boundaries better than any one else. They are indeed wonderfully expert in this matter, and unerringly point out where boundaries should run, even when the Government demarcation stones are completely overgrown by prickly-pear, or have been removed. Mr. H. A. Stuart records a custom "which prevails in some parts of making a Paraiyan walk the boundaries of a field with a pot of water on his head, when there is any dispute about their exact position." He thinks that the only satisfactory explanation of this is that the connection of the Paraiyans with the soil is "of much longer standing than that of other castes."

The admitted proprietary right which Paraiyans have in the site, known as *chēri-nattam*, on which their huts stand is a confirmation of this. These sites are entered as such on the official village maps. They cannot be taken from the Paraiyans, and date from time immemorial. Throughout the whole of the Tamil country it is usual to find that the land allotted for house-site (*nattam*) is in two portions in every village (ūr). One part is known by the Sanskrit name *grāmam* (ग्राम the village), the inhabited place). The other is called by the Dravidian name, chēri (Tam. சேரி, the gathering, or the gathering place). Sometimes the latter is called by the fuller title *parchēri*, *i.e.*, the gathering place of the Paraiyans (*Anglice* parcheri, parcherry). In the *grāmam* live the Brāhmans, who sometimes dwell in a quarter by themselves known as the *agrahāra*, and also the Kōmati Chettis, Sudra Mudaliyars, Pillais, and other Hindus. In the *paṛachēri* live the Paraiyans. The *paṛachēri* and the *grāmam* are always separated, at least by a road or lane, often by several fields.

And not only is it usual thus to find that in every village the Paraiyans as a community possess a house-site. There are many cases in which more than one *chēri* is attached to a *grāmam*. This seems to repudiate the suggestion that at some period or periods the higher castes relegated the Paraiyans to these *chēris*. Indeed in some cases the very names of the *chēris* suggest, what appears to be the more correct view, *viz.*, that the *chēris* had a distinct origin. For instance the whole revenue village (ūr) of Teiyūr near Chingleput, consists of one Sudra *grāmam* and seven Paraiya *chēris*, each with a name of its own: Periyapillēri, Komanchēri, &c. In other cases, *e.g.*, Ideipālayam to the north of the district, and Varadarajapuram near Vandalūr, only Paraiya hamlets exist; there is no *grāmam*.

In South Arcot there are at least two villages (Govindanallūr in the Chidambaram taluq and Andapet in the Tiruvanamalai taluq) inhabited only by Paraiyans, where even the maniyakkaran (munsiff, village headman) is a Paraiyan.

Other instances might be quoted in proof of the same opinion. And, when the ceremonial antipathy between Brāhman and Paraiyan is examined, it points in the same direction. It is well known that a Brāhman considers himself polluted by the touch, the presence, or the shadow of a Paraiyan, and will not allow him to enter his house, or even the street in which he lives, if it is an *agrahāra*. But it is not so well known that the Paraiyans will not allow a Brāhman to enter the *chēri*. There is more in this than the aversion of a ceremonially strict vegetarian for a degraded flesh-eating serf. Many Sudras eat mutton, but their presence does not pollute the Brāhman. The gipsy mat-makers, called Koravans and Kuruvikkārans in Tamil, and Yeṛukalas in Telugu, eat cats, rats, and even the village pig, but they are allowed to draw water from the caste wells that a Paraiyan may not look into. Mr. Padfield (*Hindu at Home*, p. 265) says that this is because the Paraiyan eats carrion. But all Paraiyans do not do so. The separation of the Paraiyan from the caste Hindu is based on a more ancient distinction than that occasional and local habit would account for.

[Should a Brahman venture into a *parachēri*, water with which cowdung has been mixed is thrown on his head, and he is driven out. Some Brahmans consider a forsaken *parachēri* an auspicious site for an agrāhāra.]

Taken together, these facts seem to show that the Paraiya priests (Valluvans), and therefore the Paraiyans as a race, are very ancient, that ten centuries ago they were respectable, and that many were weavers. The privileges they enjoy are relics of an exceedingly long association with the land. The institution of the *parachēri* points to original independence, and even to possession of much of the land.

If the account of the colonisation of Tondeimandalam by Vellālans in the eighth century A.D. is historic, then it is possible that at that date the Paraiyans lost the land, and that about that time their degradation as a race began.

I do not venture to assert for this hypothesis that it does more than fit in with such facts as are known. At any rate it bears out Dr. Oppert's conclusion that the Paraiyan is 'the representative of an ancient Dravidian population.'

N.B.—It need scarcely be said that many Paraiya hamlets are not ancient, and have come into existence through groups of Paraiyans settling on waste land. A very peculiar case is that of the *grāmam* founded for, and occupied by the clerks of the earliest Collectors (district Magistrates) of the *Jagir* of Karunguli from 1795 A.D. to 1825 A.D. These clerks were Brāhmans, and it was called the *agrahāram*. It was deserted when the head-quarters of the Collector were removed to Conjeveram. It is now occupied by Paraiyans, but is still called the *agrahāram*.

11. *A settled race.*—From this it will be clear that the Paraiyans have long been a settled race in the land. And, though a number of them emigrate to Ceylon, Mauritius, South Africa, the West Indies, the Straits Settlements, and even to Fiji, the vast majority live and die within a mile or two of the spot where they were born

12. *Their houses.*—The houses in which Paraiyans live are not temporary erections, nor intended for use during certain seasons of the year only. The rudest form is a hut made by tying a few leaves of the palmyra palm on to a frame work of poles or bamboos. The better class of houses are a series of rooms with low mud walls and thatched roof, but generally without doors, surrounding a small court-yard, in which the family goats, buffaloes and fowls have their home. The cooking is done anywhere where it is convenient either in-doors or out, as there is no fear of pollution from the glance or shadow of any passer-by. Very occasionally the walls of the house, especially those facing the street, are white-washed, or decorated with variegated patterns or figures in red and white. Paraiya women, like higher caste women, are much given to tracing exceedingly intricate symmetrical designs (Tamil *kōlam*, கோலம்) with rice flour on the smooth space or pathway immediately before the doors of their houses, for the purpose of preventing the entrance of evil spirits.

13. *Admissions to the caste.*—Admissions to the Paraiya caste from higher castes do occur. I met an Aiyangar Brâhman who was working as a cooly with some Paraiya labourers at Kodaikânal on the Palni hills. He had become infatuated with a Paraiya woman, and had consequently been excommunicated from his own caste. He had then become a Paraiyan. The children of Mudaliyar (Sudra) men and Paraiya women are considered to be Paraiyans. In Madras city many low Eurasians are supposed to have been absorbed in the ranks of the Christian, especially the Roman Catholic Paraiya population in Black Town. There are no ceremonies to be undergone before admission to the ranks of the Paraiyans.

14. *Panchayats, Paṇakkāra, Dēsayi Chettis.*—In every Paraiya village (*parchēri*) a small number of the more important men are known as *paṇakkārar* (Tamil பணக்காரன் *money-man*). The application of the term may be due to their comparative opulence among their miserable neighbours, or it may have arisen from the custom of paying them a small sum (for *panam* means a small copper coin of varying value, worth nominally eighty cowries) for various services to the commune. They form a sort of committee or council to decide ordinary quarrels, to amerce the damages in case of assault, seduction, rape and adultery. They have power to dissolve marriages on account of the adultery of

the wife, or if the husband has deserted his wife. In these cases their authority is really based on the public opinion of the *paracheri*, and goes no further than that public opinion will enforce it. A meeting of these *paṇakkārar* is called a *panchāyat, i.e.*, a meeting of a committee of five persons, but the number of *paṇakkārar* in a *panchāyat* varies. There is no headman in a Paraiya hamlet corresponding to the munsiff (Tamil *maniyakkāran* மணியக்காரன்) or village magistrate of the Hindu village (*grāma*). In modern practice the Paraiyans are, for police purposes, under the authority of the munsiff of the *grāma*, and there is a growing tendency on their part to refer all disputes and assaults to the munsiff, or even directly to the police. On the other hand, cases of a more domestic nature, such as disputes about betrothals, seduction, &c., are still dealt with, generally acutely and fairly, by the Paraiya *panchāyat*. It should be added that the rank of *paṇakkāran* is hereditary, and is regarded as honourable. (See also section 25.)

The Paraiyans like all the other 'right-hand' (*valarakei*) castes—a phrase which marks a distinction among the Dravidian castes now quite meaningless—also come under the jurisdiction of the Dēsayi Chettis, who have held a sort of censorship since the days of the Nawābs of Arcot over some twenty-four of these 'right-hand' castes, chiefly in North Arcot. The Dēsayi Chetti has nominal power to deal with all moral offences, and is supposed to have a représentative in every village, who reports every offence. But, though his authority is great in North Arcot, and the fines levied there bring in an income of hundreds of rupees yearly, it is not so much dreaded in other districts. The punishment usually inflicted is a fine; but sometimes a delinquent Paraiyan will be made to crawl on his hands and knees on the ground, between the legs of a Paraiya woman, as a final humiliation. The punishment of excommunication, *i.e.*, cutting off from fire and water, is sometimes the fate of the recalcitrant, either before the *panchāyat* or the Dēsayi Chetti; but it is seldom effective for more than a short time.

Mr. K. Rangachari adds that in certain places, the Dēsayi Chetti appoints the Pannakkāran, and that in this case the latter is subordinate to the Dēsayi, and that a man called the Variyan or Chalavāthi is sometimes appointed as assistant to the Paṇakkāran. He also mentions some other punishments. The fine for adultery is from 7 pagodas 14 fanams to 11 pagodas, when the wronged woman is unmarried. If she is married, the amount ranges from 12 pagodas 14 fanams to 16 pagodas. The fine is said to be divided between the woman, her husband, the members of the *panchāyat* and the *pannakkārans*. Formerly an offender against the Paraiyan community was tied to a post at the beginning of the trial, and, if found guilty, was beaten. He might escape the flogging by paying a fine of 2 fanams (one fanam=$2\frac{1}{2}$ annas) per stripe.

Sometimes a delinquent is paraded through the hamlet carrying a rubbish basket, or is ordered to make a heap of rubbish at a certain spot. Sometimes a cord is passed from one big toe over the bowed neck of the culprit, and tied to his other big toe and then a stone is placed on his bent back.

In some places, when an unmarried woman is convicted of adultery, she is publicly given a new cloth and a bit of straw or a twig, apparently in mockery. It is said that formerly, if the chastity of a bride was suspected, she had to pick some cakes out of boiling oil. This she had to do just after the tāli had been tied in the wedding ceremony, after bathing. Her hair, nails, and clothes were examined, to see that she had no charm concealed. After lifting the cakes from the oil, she had to husk some rice with her bare hand. If she could do this, her virtue was established.

[Excommunicated Paraiyans are said to go to a mythical place called Vinnamangalam. It is an utter insult to tell a Paraiya to go to Vinnamangalam. In some documents signed by Paraiyans the words "If I fail to fulfil the conditions of our agreement, I shall go to Vinnamangalam" are inserted.]

15. *Oaths.*—In all inquiries by the Police, the *panchāyat*, or the Dēsayi Chetti, the Paraiyan only tells what in his opinion it is expedient to tell. But evidence given after burning a piece of camphor is said to be reliable. I know no instance of trial by ordeal. (See para. 14 *ad fin.* and para. 18.)

16. *Marriage.*—As in most Eastern races, all matters relating to sex have an unhealthy prominence among Paraiyans, and no account of the Paraiyans can omit mention of the fact. The attainment of puberty by boys is not made a matter of much comment; but, in the case of girls, it is a subject of greedy curiosity to most of the women in

Plate XI.

PARAIYANS,

the village. The child at once begins to wear a covering of some sort, even if it be the most pathetic rag, over her left shoulder and breast. Till this time a bit of cotton cloth round her waist has been considered sufficient.

[Among the Tangalān Paraiyans, when a girl attains puberty, she is kept apart either in the house or in a separate hut. Pollution is supposed to last eight days. On the ninth day, the girl is bathed and seated in the court-yard of the house. Flowers and betel-leaves are placed before her. Ten small lamps of flour paste (called *drishti māvu vilakku*), to avert the evil eye, are put on a sieve, and waved before her three times. Then coloured water (*arati* or *ālām)* and burning camphor are waved before her. Some near female relatives then stand behind her, and strike her waist and sides with *puttu* (flour cake) tied in a cloth. This is believed to make her strong. At the same time other women strike the ground behind the girl with a rice-pestle. Then presents are given to the girl.

In some places the girl is beaten with the *puttu* within the house by her mother-in-law or paternal aunt. The latter repeatedly asks the girl to promise that her daughter shall marry her paternal aunt's son.]

17. *Prohibitions to marriage.*—I am not aware of any prohibitions to marriage based on social status, geographical or local differences in the places of residence, or on differences of, or changes in occupation. A village Paraiyan may marry a Paraiya woman from a town. An agricultural labourer may marry the daughter of a domestic servant. Difference in religion is also of little moment. A Christian Paraiyan will marry a heathen girl; though it should be said that she is usually baptised at or about the time of the marriage. A Christian girl is sometimes married to a heathen Paraiyan. I do not think that the fact that certain Paraiyans paint the *nāmam* of Vishnu on their foreheads, while others smear their foreheads with the ashes of Sīva, prevents marriages between them. It is said the Paraiya priests (Valluvans) marry among themselves only; but I doubt if this is so. Of course Tamil Paraiyans do not marry Telugu Pariahs (Mālas).

The man must be older than his bride. Subject to this condition, it is usual for a youth to marry his father's sister's daughter, or his mother's brother's daughter. A girl should be married to her mother's brother's son, if he is old enough, but not, as among the Konga Vellālas and some Reddis, if he is a child. In short, Paraiyans follow the usual Tamil custom, but it is often neglected.

18. *Marriage contracts.*—Marriage contracts are sometimes made by parents while the parties most concerned are still infants; often while they are still children; in the majority of cases about the time when the girl attains the marriageable age. The bridegroom may be many years older than the bride, especially when custom, as detailed above, settles who shall be his bride. The bride has absolutely no choice in the matter; but, if the bridegroom is a man of some years or position, his preferences are consulted. The older sister should be given in marriage before her younger sisters are married. The arrangements are more or less a bargain. Presents of clothes, paltry jewels, rice, vegetables, and perhaps a few rupees are exchanged between the families of the bride and of the bridegroom. The household that seeks the marriage naturally gives the larger gifts.

The actual marriage ceremony is very simple. The essential part is the tying of a small token or ornament (Tamil *tāli*, தாலி), varying in value from a few annas to four or five rupees, by a turmeric-stained string, round the neck of the bride. This is done by the bridegroom in the presence of a Valluvan (see section 30), who mutters some kind of blessing on the marriage. A series of feasts, lasting over two or three days, is given to all the relatives of both parties by the parents of newly married couple.

The bride and bridegroom do not live together immediately, even if the girl is old enough. The exact date at which their life together may begin is settled by the bride's mother. The occasion, called in Tamil *soppana-muhūrttam* (சொப்பன முகூர்த்தம்), is celebrated by another feast and much merry-making, not always seemly.

Paraiyans do not prostitute either unmarried or married women for gain as a tribal custom. Even among the most degraded, immorality is considered terribly disgraceful in a girl. In a married woman it is a matter for the husband to attend to. A Paraiya man is not expected to be chaste.

The following detailed account of the marriage ceremonies among the Tangalān Paraiyans was furnished by Mr. K. Rangachari. The parents or near relations of the contracting parties meet, and talk over the match. If an agreement is arrived at, an adjournment is made to the nearest liquor shop, and a day fixed for the formal exchange of betel leaves, which is the sign of a binding engagement. A Paraiyan, when he goes to seek the hand of a girl in marriage, will not eat at her house if her family refuse to consider the alliance, to which the consent of the girl's maternal uncle is essential. The Paraiyan is particular in the observation of omens, and, if a cat or a Valiyan crosses his path when he sets out in quest of a bride, he will give her up. The betrothal ceremony, or *pariyam*, is binding as long as the contracting couple are alive. They may live together as man and wife without performing the marriage ceremonial, and children born to them are considered as legitimate. But, when their offspring marry, the parents must first go through the marriage rites, and the children are then married in the same pandal on the same day. At the betrothal ceremony, the headman, father, maternal uncle, and two near relations of the bridegroom-elect, proceed to the girl's house, where they are received, and sit on seats or mats. Drink and plantain fruits are offered to them. Some conversation takes place between the headmen of the two parties, such as "Have you seen the girl? Have you seen her house and relations? Are you disposed to recommend and arrange the match?" If he assents, the girl's headman says "As long as stones and the Kāveri river exist, so that the sky goddess Akāsavāni and the earth goddess Bhūmidēvi may know it; so that the water-pot (used at the marriage ceremony) and the sun and moon may know it; so that this assembly may know it; I . . . . . give this girl." The headman of the bridegroom then says "The girl shall be received into the house by marriage. These thirty-six pieces of gold are yours, and the girl mine." He then hands over betel-leaves and nuts to the other headman, who returns them. The exchange of betel is carried out three times. Near the headmen is placed a tray containing betel-nuts, a rupee, a turmeric-dyed cloth in which a fanam (2¼ annas) is tied, a cocoanut, flowers, and the bride's money varying in amount from seven to twenty rupees. The fanam and bride's money are handed to the headman of the girl, and the rupee is divided between the two headmen. On the betrothal day the relations of the girl offer flowers, cocoanuts, etc., to their ancestors, who are supposed to be without food or drink. The Paraiyans believe that their ancestors will be ill-disposed towards them if they are not propitiated with offerings of rice, and other things. For the purpose of worship, the ancestors are represented by a number of cloths kept in a box made of bamboo or other material, to which the offerings are made. On the conclusion of the ancestor worship, the two headmen go to the liquor shop, and exchange drinks of toddy. This exchange is called *mel sambandham kural*, or proclaiming relationship. After the lapse of a few days, the girl's family is expected to pay a return visit, and the party should include at least seven men. Betel is again exchanged, and the guests are fed, or presented with a small gift of money. When marriage follows close on betrothal, the girl is taken to the houses of her relations, and goes through the *nalagu* ceremony, which consists of smearing her with turmeric paste, an oil-bath, and presentation of betel and sweets. The auspicious day and hour for the marriage are fixed by the Valluvan, or priest of the Paraiyans. The ceremonial is generally carried through in a single day. On the morning of the wedding day, three male and two married female relations of the bridegroom go to the potter's house, to fetch the pots, which have already been ordered. The potter's fee is a fowl, pumpkin, paddy, betel, and a few annas. The bride, accompanied by the headman and her relations, goes to the bridegroom's village, bringing with her a number of articles called *petti varisai* or box presents. These consist of a lamp, cup, brass vessel, ear-ornament called *kalappu*, twenty-five betel leaves and nuts, onions, and cakes, a lump of jaggery (palm sugar), grass mat, silver toe-ring, rice, a bundle of betel leaves, and five cocoanuts, which are placed inside a bamboo box. The next item in the proceedings is the erection of the milk-post, which is made of a pestle of tamarind or *Soymida febrifuga* wood, or a green bamboo. To the post leafy twigs of the mango or pīpal (*Ficus religiosa*) tree are tied. Near the marriage dais a pit is dug, into which are thrown nine kinds of grain, and milk is poured in. The milk-post is supported on a grinding stone painted with turmeric stripes, washed with milk and cow's urine, and worshipped, with the Valluvan as the celebrant priest. The post is then lifted by three men and two women, and set up in the pit. A string with a bit of turmeric (kankanam) is tied to the milk-post, and to it and the dais boiled rice is offered. Kankanams are also tied round the wrists of the bride and bridegroom. The bridegroom's party go to the temple or house where the bride is awaiting them, bringing with them a brass lamp, vessel and cup, castor and gingelly oil, combs, confectionary, turmeric, and betel leaves. The procession is headed by Paraiyans beating tom-toms, and blowing on trumpets. When their destination is reached, all take their seats on mats, and the various articles which they have brought are handed over to the headman, who returns them. The bride is then taken in procession to the marriage house, which she is the first to enter. She is then told to touch with her right hand some paddy, salt, and rice, placed in three pots inside the house. Touching them with the left hand would be an evil omen, and every mishap which might occur in the family would be traced to the new daughter-in-law. The bride and bridegroom next go through the nalagu ceremony, and some of the relations proceed with the ceremony of bringing sand (*manal vāri sodangu*). A cousin of the bridegroom and his wife take three pots, called *basakaragam* and *kursul*, and repair to a river, tank (pond), or well, accompanied by a few men and women. The pots are set on the ground, and close to them are placed a lamp, and a leaf with cakes, betel leaves and nuts, spread on it. *Pūja* is made to the pots by burning camphor, and breaking cocoanuts. The Vettiyan then says "The sun, the moon, the pots, and the owner of the girl have come to the pandal. So make haste, and fill the pot with water." The woman dips a small pot in water, and, after putting some sand or mud into a big pot, pours the water therein. The pots are then again worshipped. After the performance of the *nalagu*, the bridal couple go through a ceremony for removing the evil eye, called *sige kazhippu*. A leaf of *Ficus religiosa*, with its tail downwards, is held over their foreheads, and all the close relations pour milk over it, so that it trickles over their faces, or seven cakes are placed by each of the relations on the head, shoulders, knees, feet, and other parts of the body of the bridegroom. The cakes are subsequently given to a washerman. The parents of the bridal pair, accompanied by some of their relations, next proceed to an open field, taking with them the cloths, *tāli*, jewels, and other things which have been purchased for the wedding. A cloth is laid on the ground, and on it seven leaves are placed, and cooked rice, vegetables, etc., heaped up thereon. *Pūja* is done, and a goat is sacrificed to the Tangalāmmās (ancestors). By some the offerings are made to the village goddess, Pidāri, instead of to the ancestors. Meanwhile the bridegroom has been taken in procession round the village on horse-back, and the headmen have been exchanging betel in the pandal. On the bridegroom's return, he and the bride seat themselves on planks placed on the dais, and are garlanded by their maternal uncles with wreaths of *Nerium oleander* flowers. The maternal uncle of the bride presents her with a ring. In some places, the bride is carried to the dais on the shoulders, or in the arms of her maternal uncle. While the couple are seated on the dais, the Valluvan priest lights the sacred fire (hōmam), and, repeating some words in corrupt Sanskrit, pours gingelly oil on to the fire. He then does *pūja* to the *tāli*, and passes it round, to be touched and blessed by those assembled. The bridegroom, taking up the *tāli*, shows it through a hole in the pandal to the sky or sun, and, on receipt of permission from those present, ties it round the neck of the bride. Thin plates of gold or silver, called *pattam*, are then tied on the foreheads of the contracting couple, first by the mother-in-law and sister-in-law. With Brāhman and non-Brāhman castes it is customary for the bride and bridegroom to fast until the *tāli* has been tied. With Paraiyans, on the contrary, the rite is performed after a good meal. Towards the close of the marriage day, fruit, flowers, and betel are placed on a tray before the couple, and all the kankanams, seven in number, are removed, and put on the tray. After burning camphor, the bridegroom hands the tray to his wife, and it is exchanged between them three times. It is then given to a washerman. The proceedings terminate by the two going with linked hands three times round the pandal. On the following day, the bride's relations purchase some good curds, a number of plantains, sugar and pepper, which are mixed together. All assemble at the pandal, and some of the mixture is given to the headman, the newly-married couple, and all who are present. All the articles which constitute the bride's dowry are then placed in the pandal, and examined by the headman. If they are found to be correct, he proclaims the union of the couple, and more of the curd mixture is doled out. This ceremony is known as *sambandham karal* or *sammandham piriththal*, (proclaiming relationship). Two or three days after the marriage, the bridegroom goes to the house of the bride, and remains there for three days. He is stopped at the entrance by his brother-in-law, who washes his feet, puts rings on the second toe, and keeps on pinching his feet until he has extracted a promise that the bridegroom will give his daughter, if one is born to him, in marriage to the son of his brother-in-law. The ring is put on the foot of the bride by her maternal uncle at the time of the marriage ceremony, after the wrist threads have been removed. In some places it is done by the mother-in-law or sister-in-law, before the *tāli* is tied, behind a screen.

19. *Secondary wives.*—Polyandry does not exist among Paraiyans, and polygamy is not common, but I have known a few instances in which a Paraiyan had two regularly married wives, each wearing a *tāli*. On the other hand it is very common to find that a Paraiyan has, in addition to his formally married wife, another woman who occupies a recognised position in his household. The first wears the *tāli* (marriage badge). The other woman does not, but she is called 'the second wife' [Tamil (vulgar) இரண்டாவது பெண்சாதி]. She cannot be dismissed without the sanction of the *paracheri panchāyat*. The man who maintains her is called her husband, and her children are recognised as part of his family. I believe that a 'second wife' is usually taken only when the more formally married wife has no children, or when an additional worker is wanted in the house, or to help in the daily work. Thus a horsekeeper will often have two wives; one to prepare his meals and boil the grain for the horse, the other to go out day by day to collect grass for the horse. The Tamil proverb இரண்டு பெஞ்சாதிக்காரன் பாடு திண்டாட்டம், *i.e.*, "The experience of a man with two wives is anguish" applies to all these double unions. There are constant quarrels between the two women, and the man is generally involved, often to his own great inconvenience.

So far as I know, there is no prohibition against a Paraiyan marrying two sisters, either formally, or in the less regular manner just detailed. But this is not very common, unless the elder sister dies. Should she do so, it is quite common for a Paraiyan to marry his deceased wife's sister, if she is not already married.

20. *Births.*—A Paraiya woman usually goes back to her mother's house a month or two before she expects the birth of her first child; and it is usually born there. Its successors are generally born in their father's hut. I know of no special customs observed by the father or mother when the child is expected. Paraiya women are often very muscular, and engage in field-work to within a day to two, sometimes till within an hour or two of their confinement. The young wife's mother, and the women of the village look after her. Sometimes a "medicine-woman" (Tamil *maruttuvacchi*, மருத்துவச்சி), who possesses or professes some knowledge of drugs and midwifery, is called in, if the case

is a bad one. Generally her barbarous treatment is but additional torture to the patient.

No special ceremonies are performed at the birth of a child; nor, so far as I know, is the mother subjected to any special diet, though for some days she lives chiefly on *kanji* (Tamil கஞ்சி, the water in which rice has been boiled, a kind of weak rice-broth). Immediately after the birth of the child, she drinks a concoction called *kashāyam* (Tamil கஷாயம்), in which there is much ginger. (Hence the Tamil proverb சுக்கு அறியாத கஷாயம் உண்டா, Is there any decoction without ginger in it?)

21. *Simanta.*—Among Sūdras there is a family ceremony to which the Sanskrit name *Simanta* has been assigned, though it is not the true *Simanta* observed by Brāhmans. It occurs only in connection with a first pregnancy. The expectant mother stands bending over a rice-mortar, and water, or human milk, is poured on her back by her husband's elder or younger sister. Money is also given to buy jewels for the expected child. The ceremony is of no interest to any one outside the family. (Hence the proverb ஊராரே வாருங்கள் முதுகு நீர் குத்துங்கள், Come ye villagers, pour water on this woman's back!) This is used when outsiders are called in to dc for a member of a family what the relatives ought to do. I have known this ceremony to be observed among Paraiyans, but not commonly. Among Brāhmans it is believed to affect the sex of the child. I doubt whether it has any definite meaning among Paraiyans. About a week after the birth of her child, the mother, as a purificatory ceremony, is rubbed with oil and bathed. She then returns to her regular duties in the house.

It should be added that it is firmly believed that, if a woman dies during pregnancy or in childbed, her spirit becomes an exceedingly malignant ghost, and haunts the precincts of the village where she dies.

I know of no special beliefs or customs with regard to twins or monstrosities. My impression is that it is not at all common for a Paraiya woman to have twins; but there is no possibility of verifying this.

22. *Naming.*—There is no special ceremony for naming a child among Paraiyans, as far as I know. Apparently its parents choose a name for it, or it receives a name by accident. Frequently its only name is a nick-name, which serves it all its life. (See section 8.)

23. *Widows.*—The widow of a Paraiyan, if not too old to bear children, generally lives with another man as his wife. Sometimes she is ceremonially married to him, and then wears the *tāli* (see section 18). So far as I have observed, a widow practically chooses her own second husband, and she is not restricted to any particular relative, such as her husband's elder or younger brother. The practice of the Levirate, by which the younger brother takes the widow of the elder, is non-existent as a custom among Paraiyas, though instances of such unions may bo found. Indeed the popular opinion of the Tamil castes credits the Paraiyan with little regard for any of the restrictions of consanguinity, either prohibitive or permissive. "The palmyra palm has no shadow: the Paraiyan has no regard for seemliness." (பனைமரத்திற்கு நிழல் இல்லை, பறையனுக்கு முறையில்லை) is a common Tamil proverb.

During her widowhood a woman does not wear her *tāli*. It is removed at a gathering of her relatives some days after her husband's death. Paraiya women do not wear any distinctive dress when they are widows; nor do they shave their heads. But they cease to paint the vermilion mark (Tam. *kunkumam*) on their foreheads, which all married women who are living with their husbands always wear, except at times when they are considered ceremonially unclean.

24. *Divorce.*—Divorce is permitted. Frequently man and wife separate without any formality; but, where property is affected, the matter is referred to the *panchāyat* (see section 14). Both parties or their relatives are present at these inquiries, and usually fairly equitable decisions are arrived at. Adultery is not treated with the same severity by a Paraiya *panchāyat* as by the Canon Law, and is frequently compounded by a small fine. A wife, whose divorce has been sanctioned by the *panchāyat*, may be formally married again to her new lover, and wear the *tāli* of honourable married life.

25. *Inheritance.*—When a Paraiyan dies, his property, if he has any, descends to his family, as a family, according to ordinary Hindu usage. A mother's jewels generally pass to her daughter. Sometimes property, especially land, is divided on the death of the head of an household. In this case, his widow (if he leaves one) and his children, male and female, have shares more or less equal, according to an arrangement agreed upon by them, and settled by the

panchāyat. Inheritance of any petty communal office, such as watchman (*Talayāri*), digger (*Vettiyan*) is through the male. If there is more than one son, the sons hold the place, and take its emoluments in rate-free land and gifts from the villagers by turns for certain periods.

26. *Religion.*—The Report on the Census of 1891 says : " The Paraiyans have been but little affected by Brāhmanical doctrines and customs, though in respect to ceremonies they have not escaped their influence. Paraiyans are nominally Saivites, but in reality they are demon-worshippers." This is a very incomplete account of the religion of the Paraiyan, and is not entirely correct.

Brāhman influence has scarcely affected the Paraiyan at all, even in ceremonial. No Paraiyan may enter any Vaishnava or Saiva temple even of the humblest sort, though of course his offerings of money are accepted, if presented by the hands of some friendly Sudra, even in such exclusive shrines as that of Sri Vira Rāghavachāriar Swāmi at Tiruvallūr. The exceptions mentioned in section 10 confirm this by their uniqueness.

It is true that Paraiyans are often termed Saivites, but there are many nominal Vaishnavas among them, who regularly wear the *nāmam* of Vishnu on their foreheads. The truth is that the feminine deities, commonly called *dēvata* (*i.e.*, spirits, *ηαωρωοζια* outside the vedic, epic and puranic pantheons) have been identified by Hindus with the feminine energy of Sīva ; and thus the Paraiyans who worship them have received the sectarian epithet. (See section 27.) As a matter of fact, the wearing of the *nāmam* of Vishnu, or the smearing of the ashes of Sīva, is of no meaning to a Paraiyan. They are neither Saivites nor Vaishnavites.

One other fact also must be allowed to modify the statement that Paraiyans are demon-worshippers. Like all other Dravidians, the Paraiyans acknowledge the existence of a supreme, omnipresent, personal spiritual being, the source of all, whom they call *Kadavul* (கடவுள், *i.e.*, He who is). *Kadavul* possesses no temples, and is not worshipped ; but he is the highest conception of Paraiya, and, I believe, of Dravidian thought.

27. *Dēvata.*—Paraiyans worship at least *three* classes of godlings or *dēvata* (Tamil தேவதே), generally called " the mothers," (Tamil *amma*, அம்மன், அம்மா, அம்மாள்).

Plate XII.

PARAIYANS.

Sometimes these are worshipped as "the virgins" (Tamil *Kanniyamma* கன்னியம்மாக்கள்) or "the seven virgins," possibly because they have no husband.

(i) These "mothers" are worshipped collectively, in a group. They are then symbolised by seven stones or bricks, perhaps within a little enclosure, or on a little platform in the Paraiya hamlet, or under a margosa tree (Hind. nīm, Tam. வேம்பு), or sheltered by a wattle hut, or even by a small brick temple. This temple is universally known as the *Ammankoil* (Tam. அம்மன்கோவில்).

(ii) More usually one particular "mother" is worshipped at the Paraiya shrine. She is then called the village goddess (Tam. கிராம தேவதை, Sanskrit *grāma-dēvatā*) of that particular hamlet. She may be identical with the *grāma-dēvatā* of the Hindus living in the *grāmam*, or she may not. In any case she has her own shrine in the Paraiyan's hamlet. These "mothers" have no individuality. Their names are legion. Each village claims that its own "mother" is not the same as that of the next village; but all are supposed to be sisters. Each is supposed to be the guardian of the boundaries of the *chēri* or *grāmam* where her temple lies, sometimes of both *grāmam* and *chēri*. She is believed to protect its inhabitants and its live-stock from disease, disaster and famine, to promote the fecundity of cattle and goats, and to give children. In a word she is the benefactress of the place, and of all in it who worship her.

The following are a few of the names of these village tutelary deities:—

Ellammā : goddess of the boundary. She is worshipped by Tamil and Telugu Paraiyans.

Mūngilammā : bamboo goddess.

Padeiyattāl or *Padeiyācchi.*

Parrapotamma. She is a Telugu goddess supposed to cure diseases among cattle.

Pidārīyammā. Sometimes called Ellei-Pidāri.

In this case the symbol of the goddess may be a conical stone or a carved idol. The shrine is the same as that described above. Occasionally a rude figure of the bull Nandi, and an iron trident mark the shrine. A lamp is often lighted before it at night.

The ceremonial of worship of all classes of *dēvata* is very simple. The worshipper prostrates himself before the symbol of the deity (whether seven stones, one stone, or an image). He anoints it with oil, smears it with saffron, and daubs it with vermilion, garlands it with flowers (*Nerium odorum*, by preference) burns a bit of camphor, and circumambulates the shrine, keeping his right side toward it.

On special occasions he breaks cocoanuts, kills fowls, goats or sheep, of which the two last must be killed at one blow, pours out their blood, perhaps offers a little money, and goes his way, satisfied that he has done his best to propitiate the *dēvata* whom he has honoured

28. *Festival at Periyapālayam.*--Of course special shrines attain very great fame. Thus the goddess Bavāniyammāl of Periyapālayam, some sixteen miles from Madras, is well known for many miles round, and crowds come from Madras city and even more distant places to her annual festival. Paraiyans, Pallis, and Chakkiliyans form the majority of the worshippers, but of late years Sudras and even Brāhmans are to be found at her shrine. The homage rendered to her is two-fold. Her worshippers sacrifice some thousands of sheep on the river bank outside her temple; and, entirely divesting themselves of their garments, and covering themselves with bunches of the leaves of the nīm or margosa (*Melia Azadirachta*) tree, perambulate the temple. Except on the five Sundays, usually in July and August, on which the festival is held, the shrine is forsaken, and the goddess is said to be a vegetarian; but on the five festival Sundays she is said to be as greedy for flesh as a leather-dresser's (Chakkiliyan) wife. A legend is told to account for this, which is practically as follows:—

There was once a *rishi*, who lived on the banks of the Periyapālayam river with his wife Bavani. Every morning she used to bathe in the river, and bring back water for the use of the household. But she never took any vessel with her in which to bring the water home, for she was so chaste that she had acquired power to form a water-pot out of the dry river sand, and carry the water home in it. But one day, while bathing, she saw the reflection of the face of the sky-god Indra in the water, and could not help admiring it. When she returned to the bank of the river, and tried to form her water-pot out of sand, as usual, she could not do so, for her admiration of Indra had ruined her power, and she went home sadly to fetch a brass water-vessel. Her husband saw her carrying this to the river, and at once suspected her of unchastity. Calling his son, he ordered him to strike off her head with a sword. It was in vain that the son tried to avoid matricide. He had to obey, but he was so agitated by his feelings that, when at last he struck at his mother, he cut off not only her head, but also that of a leather-dresser's wife who was standing near. The two bodies lay side by side. The *rishi* was so pleased with his son's obedience that he promised him any favour that he should ask, but he was very angry when the son at once begged that his mother might be restored to life. Being compelled to keep his word, he told the son that, if he put his mother's head on her trunk, she would again live. The son tried to do so, but in his haste took up the head of the leather-dresser's wife by mistake, and put that to Bavani's body. Leather-dressers are flesh eaters, and so it comes about that on the days when her festival is celebrated Bavani—now a goddess—longs for meat, and thousands of sheep, goats, and fowls must be slain at her shrine. This legend bears marks of Brāhmanic influence. Curiously enough the priest of this Paraiya shrine is himself a Brāhman.

I am unable to give any explanation of the wearing of the margosa leaves. The people do it in fulfilment of a vow made in time of their own sickness, or that of their children, or even of their cattle. Thus a woman ill of fever will vow "to wear margosa leaves at Periyapālayam" if she recover. The vow may be made on behalf of a sick cow, and the animal will be bathed in the river, clad in margosa leaves, and led round the temple like any other worshipper. The act is thus a thanksgiving for mercies received, not an attempt to propitiate the goddess.

It should be noted that Periyapālayam is one of the shrines where hook-swinging was practised. The apparatus still lies beside the temple.

29. *Māriyattāl and Gangammāl.*—Two goddesses hold a position distinct from the "mothers" as a group, or as tutelary goddesses. These are Gangammāl and Māriyattāl, and their peculiarity is that they are itinerant deities. Gangammāl is often described as the goddess of cholera, and Māriyattāl as the goddess of small-pox, though both diseases are frequently ascribed to the latter. Māriyattāl is worshipped under the names of Poleramma (పోలేరమ్మ), and Ammavāru (అమ్మవారు) by Telugus. Sūdras as well as Paraiyans worship these deities.

For instance, near Arcotkuppam in the North Arcot district, a festival is held in honour of Gangammāl in the Tamil month *Vaikasi* (May–June), in which Sūdras join. The feature of the festival is the boiling of new rice as at Pongal. Men also put on women's clothes, and perform grotesque dances. In the same way, in the ten days' festival in honour of Māriyattāl held at Urtaramallūr during the Tamil month *Avani* (August), the goddess is carried about by washermen (Vannān), who perform a kind of pantomime (*vilas*), in her honour.

There is a curious belief that these goddesses (or Gangammāl, if they are distinguished) must travel along roads or paths, and cannot go across country, and that they cannot pass over the leaves of the margosa or the stems of the cactus called in Tamil perandei. Consequently, when cholera is about, and the goddess is supposed to be travelling from village to village seeking victims, branches of margosa and long strings of *perandei* are cut and placed on all the paths leading into *grāmam* or *chēri*. Sometimes, also, leaves of the margosa are strung together, and hung across the village street. These are called *toranam*.

Besides the various deities thus enumerated, there are a number of ghosts, ghouls and goblins (Tamil *pey*, *pisāsu* பேய், பிசாசு) that Paraiyans propitiate more or less regularly. Mathureivīran and Vīrabadran are two well-known demons. Also the ghosts of women who have died in child-bed come under this category.

30. *Paraiya priests or Valluvans.*—Among Tamil Paraiyans and Telugu Mālas, there are families in almost every village, who hold a kind of sacerdotal rank in the esteem of their fellows. Among the Mālas they are known as the Dāsari (దాసరి). Among the Paraiyans they are called Valluvans (வள்ளுவன்); also Valluva Pandāram (வள்ளுவ பண்டாரம்), *i.e.*, the priestly Valluvan; also Valluva Paraiyan (வள்ளுவப் பறையன்), *i.e.*, the Paraiya Valluvan. I do not know what 'Valluvan' means. It is now used simply as an appellative. Their position and authority depend largely on their own astuteness. Sometimes they are respected even by Brāhmans for their powers as exorcists. On the other hand it is often impossible to see any difference between the Valluvans and the ordinary Paraiyans, except that their houses are usually a little apart from other houses in the *chēri*. They take a leading part in local Paraiya festivals.

At marriages they pronounce the formal blessing when the *tāli*, or marriage token, is tied round the bride's neck (see section 18). In cases of supposed possession by demons (பேய், பிசாசு) or by the 'mothers' (see section 27), the Valluvan is consulted as to the meaning of the portent, and takes part in driving the spirit out of the victim, sometimes using violence and blows to compel the spirit to deliver its message and be gone. The Census Report for 1901 states that Valluvans do not eat or intermarry with other sections of the Paraiyans. I am unable to confirm this, and am inclined to doubt whether it is generally true. The total number of Valluvans, according to the Census of 1901, in the Madras Presidency was 54,760. The greatest of all Tamil poets, known only as Tiruvalluvar, *i.e.*, the holy Valluvan, was a Paraiyan of this sect (see section 10).

31. *Funerals.*—Among Paraiyans the dead are buried; though a few (generally Vaishnavas, I believe), burn the corpses. A portion of the village waste land is allotted for the purpose. Only Paraiyans are buried in it. The funeral-rites are absolutely simple. The corpse is carried on a temporary litter of palm-leaf mats and bamboos, wrapped in a cotton cloth, which is new if a new one can be afforded, and is interred or burned immediately.

N.B.—I am informed that Mālas in Bellary and Anantapur bury their dead quite naked.

About the third or fifth day after death, the *pāl śadangu* (Tamil, பால்சடங்கு), or 'milk ceremony' should take place, when some milk is poured out by the next of kin as an offering to the spirit of the deceased. This spirit is then supposed to assume a sort of corporiety, and to depart to the place of respite, till fate decrees that it be re-born. Of course this ceremony is accompanied by a family feast.

On the fifteenth day after death, another family gathering is held, and food is offered to the spirit of the dead person. This ceremony is known as the *karumāntaram* (Tamil கருமாந்தரம்), or 'expiatory ceremony'.

Occasionally, for some months after the death, a few flowers are placed on the grave, and a cocoanut is broken over it, and some attempt is even made to recognise the anniversary of the date. But there is no regular custom, and I am inclined to think that such instances as I have noticed are imitations of Brāhmanical usages.

The ordinary Paraiyan's conception of life after death is merely a vague belief that the departed soul continues its existence somewhere. He has no ordered eschatology.

The bodies are placed in the grave in a horizontal position. I know of no instance of their being buried in a sitting position; though it is very likely that the corpse of a Paraiyan who has acquired reputation for sanctity—as some do—may be buried in a sitting posture, like Sanyāsis. Valluvans are buried in a sitting position.

Children are buried in the usual way in the ordinary burial-ground. But, if the first-born child *is a male*, it is buried by the house, or even within the house, so that its corpse may not be carried off by any witch or sorcerer, to be used in magic rites (சூனியம்), as the body of a first-born child is supposed to possess special virtues. This practice, which is known in other castes besides the Paraiyans, was brought to my notice by the Rev. W. Goudie of Tiruvallūr about three years ago.

Mr. V. Govindan of the Madras Museum, has supplied the following note on the death ceremonies of the Paraiyans at Coimbatore. If the deceased was a married man, the corpse is placed in a sitting posture in a booth made of twigs of margosa (*Melia Azadirachta*) and milk-hedge (*Euphorbia Tirucalli*), and supported behind by a mortar. The widow puts on all her ornaments, and decorates her hair with flowers. She seats herself on the left side of the corpse, in whose hands some paddy (unhusked rice) or salt is placed. Taking hold of its hands, some one pours the contents thereof into the hands of the widow, who replaces them in those of the corpse. This is done thrice, and the widow then ties the rice in her cloth. On the way to the burial-ground (*sudukādu*), the son carries a new pot, the barber a pot of cooked rice and brinjals (fruit of *Solanum Melongena*), and other things required for doing *pūja*. The Paraiyan in charge of the burial-ground carries a fire-brand. The mats and other articles used by the deceased, and the materials of which the booth were made, are carried in front by the washerman, who deposits them at a spot between the house of the deceased and the burial-ground called the *idukādu*, which is made to represent the shrine of Arichandra. Arichandra was a king, who became a slave of the Paraiyans, and is in charge of the burial-ground. At the *idukādu* the corpse is placed on the ground, and the son, going thrice round it, breaks the pot of rice near its head. The barber makes a mark at the four corners of the bier, and the son places a quarter-anna on three of the marks, and some cow-dung on the mark at the north-east corner. The widow seats herself at the feet of the corpse, and another widowed woman breaks her tāli string, and throws it on the corpse. Arrived at the grave, the *gurukal* (priest) descends into it, does *pūja*, and applies *vibhūthi* (sacred ashes) to its sides. The body is lowered into it, and half a yard of cloth from the winding-sheet is given to the Paraiyan, and a quarter of a yard to an Āndi (religious mendicant). The grave is filled in up to the neck of the corpse, and bael (*Ægle Marmelos*) leaves, salt, and *vibhūthi* are placed on its head by the *gurukal.* The grave is then filled in, and a stone and thorny branch placed at the head end. As the son goes, carrying the water-pot, three times round the grave, the barber makes a hole in the pot, which is thrown on the stone. The son and other relations bathe, and return to the house, where a vessel containing milk is set on a mortar, and another containing water placed at the door. They dip twigs of the pīpal (*Ficus religiosa*) into the milk, and throw them on the roof. They also worship a lighted lamp. On the third day, cooked rice, and other food for which the deceased had a special liking, are taken to the grave, and placed on plantain leaves. *Pūja* is done, and the crows are attracted to the spot. If they do not turn up, the *gurukal* prays, and throws up water three times. On the seventeenth day, the son and others, accompanied by the *gurukal*, carry a new brick, and articles required for *pūja*, to the river. The brick is placed under water, and the son bathes. The articles for *pūja* are spread on a plantain leaf, before which the son places the brick. *Pūja* is done to it, and a piece of new cloth tied on it. It is then again carried to the river, and immersed therein. The ceremonial concludes with the lighting of the sacred fire (hōmam).

The death ceremonies of the Paraiyan, as carried out in the Chingleput district, are thus described by Mr. K. Rangachari. The corpse is washed, dressed up, and carried on a bier to the burning or burial-ground. Just before it is placed on the bier, all the relations who are under pollution go round it three times, carrying an iron measure, round which straw has been wrapped, and containing a light. On the way to the burial-ground, the son or grandson scatters paddy (rice) which has been fried by the agnates (*pangālis*). A pot of fire is carried by a Vettiyan. At a certain spot the bier is placed on the ground, and the son goes round it, carrying a pot of cooked rice, which he breaks near the head of the corpse. This rice should not be touched by man or beast, and it is generally buried.

When the corpse has been placed on the pyre or laid in the grave, rice is thrown over it by the relations. The son, carrying a pot of water, goes round it thrice, and asks those assembled if he may finish the ceremony. On receiving their assent, he again goes three times round the corpse, and, making three holes in the pot, throws it down, and goes home without looking back. If the dead person is unmarried, a mock marriage ceremony, called *kanni kaziththal* (removing bachelorhood), is performed before the corpse is laid on the bier. A garland of arka (*Calotropis gigantea*) flowers and leaves is placed round its neck, and balls of mud from a gutter are laid on the head, knees, and other parts of the body. In some places a variant of the ceremony consists in the erection of a mimic marriage booth which is covered with leaves of the arka plant, flowers of which are also placed round the neck as a garland. On the third day after death, cooked rice, milk, fruits, etc., are offered to the soul of the departed on two leaves placed one near the head, the other near the feet of the corpse. Of these, the former is taken by men, and the latter by women, and the food eaten. The *karmānthirum*, or final ceremony, takes place on the twelfth or sixteenth day. All concerned in it proceed to a tank with cooked rice, cakes, etc. A figure of Ganēsa (*Pillayār*) is made with mud, and five *kalasams* (vessels) are placed near it. The various articles which have been brought are set out in front of it. Two bricks, on which the figures of a man and woman are drawn, are given to the son, who washes them, and does *pūja* to them after an effigy has been made at the waterside by a washerman. He then says: "I gave calves and money. Enter kailāsam (the abode of Siva). Find your way to paralōkam (the other world). I gave you milk and fruit. Go to the world of the dead. I gave gingelly (*Sesamum*) and milk. Enter yamalōkam (abode of the god of death). Eleven descendants on the mother's side and ten on the father's, twenty-one in all, may they all enter heaven." He then puts the bricks into the water. On their return home, the sons of the deceased are presented with new clothes.

32. *Totemism, &c.*—So far as I am aware, there is no trace of totemism among Pariyans. Nor do they make fire by friction or flint and steel, though they know how to use flints, but borrow glowing ashes from one another's hearths, should their own fire have gone out.

33. *Tattooing* is practised on women and children of both sexes, but not on grown men. With children the operation is confined to a simple line drawn down the forehead. Among Paraiyans who have become Roman Catholics, the device is sometimes a cross. Women frequently have their arms elaborately tattooed, and sometimes have a small pattern over the breast bone, between the breasts. This tattooing is performed in a primitive fashion. The skin is pricked till the blood comes, and a little blue pigment is rubbed in. The general effect is not unpleasant.

34. *Dress.*—The male Paraiyan wears the invariable loin-cloth, and a strip of white cotton cloth, which he may wrap round his waist, roll into a sort of turban, or hang over his shoulders. On great occasion he wears a large turban, and white cotton cloths both round his waist and over his shoulders. The use of any kind of sandal is rare.

The Paraiya woman's dress is a cotton cloth about 48 inches wide, and as long, as gorgeous and as costly as she can afford. This she winds round her waist, bringing one end up from her waist in front, over her bosom and left shoulder, and tucking it in at her waist behind. Small children wear no clothes. Boys begin to wear a loin-cloth, and girls a rag round their waists when they are about five years old. As soon as a girl is eleven or twelve, she begins to wear a corner of this rag across her bosom (see section 16).

35. *Hair.*—Paraiya men have their beards and the hair on the fore part of the head shaved as often as they can afford the luxury. But occasionally they allow their beards and hair to grow, and offer it at the shrine of some favourite deity. Ordinarily moustaches, and the hair at the back of the head are worn. The latter is usually twisted into a knot at the back of the head called in Tamil *kudumi* (குடுமி).

Women wear their hair parted in the middle of the head and gathered into a bundle (கொண்டை) behind the left ear, frequently supplementing it by wisps of false hair, which are sold openly in the bazaars. This chignon is always worn more to the left than to the right, and is ornamented with flowers on high days. But ordinarily a Paraiya woman allows her hair to remain a frowsy tumbled knot, carelessly gathered together at the back of her head.

Widows do not have their heads shaved.

Girls wear their hair as nature allows it to grow, but the heads of boys are shaved very early, and afterwards at irregular intervals. Paraiya women usually have the hair in the arm-pits shaven.

It is scarcely necessary to add that the barber, himself a Paraiyan, who shaves Paraiyans, shaves none of the higher castes.

36. *Charms and ornaments; Scare-crows.*—The small ornament called *tāli* in Tamil, worn round the necks of married women, is the only significant ornament. It indicates that a woman is formally married (see section 19), and that her husband is alive, for it is removed from the neck of a widow.

Sometimes an *arei-mūdi*, shaped like the leaf of the *pūvarasa* tree, (*Thespesia populnea*) made of silver or of silvered brass, is tied round the waist of female infants as an ornament. It has no significance.

Small flat plates of copper called *takudu* (தகடு), about one and-a-half inches square, costing a *periya panam*, *i.e.*, two and-a-half annas, are frequently worn by children. One side is divided into sixteen squares, in which what look like the Telugu numerals for nine, ten, eleven and twelve are engraved. On the other side a circle is drawn, which is divided into eight segments, in each of which a Telugu letter is inscribed. The precise meaning of these letters was unknown to my informants, but the charm is supposed to protect the wearer from harm coming from any of the eight cardinal points of the Indian compass.

Various other charms, generally small metal cylinders, are worn for the same purpose by adults and children. They are procured from some exorcist (Tam. *mantirakkāran*).

Similar, or the same charms are worn to avoid the baneful influence of the 'evil eye.' To prevent the evil eye from affecting their crops, Paraiyans put up scare-crows in their fields. These are usually small broken earthen pots, whitewashed, or covered with spots of whitewash, or even adorned with huge clay noses and ears, and made

Plate XIII.

PARAIYANS.

into grotesque faces. These are set up on the end of a pole, to attract the eye of the passer-by from the crop. For the same reason more elaborate figures made of mud and twigs, in human shape, are sometimes set up.

Before wells are sunk, a charmer (Tam. *mantirakkāran*) is called in to recite spells and find a likely spot, cocoanuts are broken, and the milk in them poured out to propitiate the gods of the place.

37. *Occupation.*—The inscription referred to by Mr. Francis (see section 10 (3)) shows that in the eleventh century A.D., Paraiyans were divided into weavers and ploughmen. To-day Paraiyans are agricultural labourers, mostly men without land. Till a score or so of years ago some were actual bond-serfs, and there are instances on record in quite recent years which show that it was no infrequent thing for a Paraiyan to mortgage his son as security for the repayment of a loan. On the other hand some Paraiya families still own much land.

Current Tamil speech and custom divide the landless labouring Paraiyans into *padiyāl* and *kūliyāl.* The *padiyāl* is definitely and hereditarily attached to some land-holding family in the Hindu *grāma* ; he can work for no one else ; and cannot change masters. His privilege is that in times of drought and famine his master must support him. The *kūliyāl* is a mere day labourer, only employed, and therefore only receiving pay (*kūli*), when required. He has no claim for maintenance in seasons of scarcity ; and thus, though no man's serf, he is far worse off than the *padiyāl.* There is, I fear, much reason to believe that there is a tendency on the part of Hindu land-owners to rid themselves of *padiyāls.*

Three communal servants—the digger, *i.e.*, the grave-digger (veṭṭiyan, வெட்டியான்), the watchman (taleiyāri, தலையாரி), and the scavenger (*toṭṭi*, தோட்டி)—are all Paraiyans. The last is regarded as of lower rank than the others. The Veṭṭiyan officiates when a corpse is buried, and also when it is burned. Hence the proverb against meddling in what ought to be left to some one else : Let the Veṭṭiyan and the corpse struggle together (வெட்டியானும் பிணமும் கட்டிப்புரளட்டும்).

in and near large towns, many Paraiyans are horse-keepers, grass-cutters, drivers, domestic servants, and day labourers at all kinds of manual work.

38. *Food.*—The staple food of the Paraiyan is rice, eaten in the usual South Indian fashion with pepper-water, tamarind, garlic, ginger, vegetables, and indeed any condiment or curry that he can get. A kind of millet, called in Tamil *kervaragu*, but more generally known as *rāgi*, (*Eleusine Coracana*) is also used by many, especially when rice is dear. All Paraiyans eat mutton, dried fish, fresh tank fish, pork, and ordinary birds that can be snared or shot, and of course fowls.

Some Paraiyans eat carrion. I have known them even dig up a buffalo that had been buried for several hours, and devour it (see section 10). It is said that even the lowest Paraiyans do not eat the flesh of cows, but leave that to the leather-dressers (Chakkiliyans). Paraiyans do not eat snakes, lizards, rats, or other vermin. In times of famine I have known them dig into ant-hills to rob the ants of their store of grass seeds. This is called 'grass-rice' (Tam. *pilarisi*, பிலரிசி). All Paraiyans drink fermented palm-juice (Tam. *Kallu*, கல்லு; anglice, 'toddy.') and also arrack when they can afford it.

39. *Proverbs about Paraiyans.*—There are many proverbs in Tamil referring to Paraiyans. Some are used by the Paraiyans about themselves. All seem to be used by the higher castes. The point of most of them lies in their allusion to the Paraiyans' degraded condition. Most of them are in Jensen's *Tamil Proverbs*. The others are in Lazarus' *Dictionary of Tamil Proverbs*. The translations and notes are Mr. Jensen's or my own.

(1) பறையன் பொங்கலிட்டால் பகவானுக்கு ஏறாதா?
If a Paraiyan boils rice, will it not reach God?
i.e., God will notice all piety, even that of a Paraiyan.

(2) பறைச்சி வெற்றிலைபோட்டால் பத்துவிரலும் சுண்ணாம்பு.
When a Paraiya woman eats betel, her ten fingers (will be daubed with) lime.
The Paraiya woman is a proverbial sloven.

(3) பறைச்சி பிள்ளையைப் பள்ளிக்கு வைத்தாலும் பேச்சிலே அய்யே என்னுமாம்.

Though a Paraiya woman's child be put to school, it will say *Ayyé* in its talk.

Ayyé is vulgar Tamil for *Aiyar*, meaning "Sir."

(4) பறைச்சேரி மேளம் கலியாணத்துக்கும் கொட்டும், கல்லெடுப்புக்கும் கொட்டும்.

The drum from the Paraiya village beats for wedding and for funerals.

Beating the drum for public notices and ceremonies is part of the work of the Veṭṭiyan.

(5) பனைமரத்திற்கு நிழலில்லை, பறையனுக்கு முறையில்லை.

The palmyra palm has no shadow; the Paraiyan has no decency.

A contemptuous reference to Paraiya morality.

(6) இருந்த நாள் எல்லாம் இருந்தவிட்டு, ஊர்ப்பறையனுக்குத் தார வார்த்ததுபோல.

Like letting something remain for a long time, and then pouring water on the village Paraiyan's hands (to take it away).

தார வார்க்க is the ceremony of pouring water into the hands of the accepter of a gift in token of donation.

(7) சுரைப்பூவுக்கும் பறைப்பாட்டுக்கும் வாசனையில்லை.

The gourd flower and the Paraiyan's song have no savour.

Paraiyans use this saying about their own singing.

(8) நண்டு கொழுத்தால் வளையிலே இராது, பறையன் கொழுத்தால் பாயிலே இரான்.

If the crab gets fat, it will not stay in its hole; if the Paraiyan gets fat, he will not stay on his mat.

This proverb appears in other forms, but this is how I have heard it quoted by Paraiyans.

(9) பட்டால் தெரியும் பறையனுக்கு.

If he suffers, a Paraiyan will get sense.

(10) எழுபது சென்றாலும் பறை ஏவினால்தான் செய்யும்.

Though seventy years of age, a Paraiyan will only do what he is compelled.

N.B. பறை is here translated பறையன்.
It might be translated "a drum."

(11) பத்துவிதத்திலும் பறையனை நம்பலாம், பார்ப்பானை நம்பக்கூடாது.

You may believe a Paraiyan, even in ten ways; you cannot believe a Brāhman.

Almost the only saying in favonr of the Paraiyan.

(12) என் பறையா என்கிறதை விட, வள்ளுவபறையா என்கிறது மேல்.

What better is it to say 'Valluva Paraiyan' than to say 'Paraiyan'?

i.e., Both are Paraiyans.

See section 30.

(13) ஆயிரம் குதிரையை அறவெட்டின சிப்பாய்தானா இப்போது பறைச்சேரி நாயோடே பங்கமழிகிருன்.

Is the sepoy, who massacred a thousand horse, now living in disgrace with the dogs of the parachēri?

(14) சைவ முத்தையாமுதலியாருக்கு சமைத்துப்போட வள்ளுவ பண்டாரம்.

A Paraiya priest is cook to the vegetarian Muttaiya Mudaliyār!

A reference to the meat-eating habits of the Paraiyans.

(15) வெட்டியானும் பிணமும் கட்டிப்புரளட்டும்.

Let the grave digger and the corpse struggle together.

See section 37.

(16) அதிகாரி வீட்டிலே திருடி தலையாரி வீட்டிலே வைத்ததுபோல்.

Like stealing from the headman's house, and putting (the stolen goods) into the house of the watchman!

See section 37.

(17) ஒளிக்கப்போயும் தலையாரி வீட்டிலா?

If you want to hide yourself, should you go to the watchman's house?

See section 37.

(18) அதிகாரியும் தலையாரியும் கூடி விடியுமட்டும் திருடலாம்.

If the headman and the watchman combine, they can steal till dawn!

See section 37.

(19) தன் பெண்சாதியைத்தான் அடிக்கத் தலையாரியைச் சீட்டுக் கேட்கிறதா?

If one wants to beat his wife, does he ask permission from the watchman?

(20) பறைப்பேச்சு அரைப்பேச்சு.

Paraiyan's talk is half talk.

A reference to Paraiya vulgarisms of speech. See section 6.

(21) பறையனும் பார்ப்பானும் போல.

Like Pariah and Brāhman.

i.e., As different from each other as possible.

INDEX.

[The numbers refer to the sections.]

THE LEGEND OF NANDAN.

[Translated from the prose version in the *Periyapūrana Vasanam* by the Rev. A. C. CLAYTON.]

"There was a man named Nandan, a Pulaiyan by caste, living in Athanur, in the Melkā district on the banks of the Kollidam (Coleroon) river in the kingdom of the Chōlas. He forget all other things, and would only think on the holy feet of the Supreme Sīva (*Paramasivan*). Because he was a grave-digger, he made a living by the crop that grew in the portion of land that was the perquisite of the man who did the grave-digging in that village, and did the work he ought to do. He provided the skin and the sinews for stretching the skin on the *perikei* (a drum made by stretching skin over a large iron bowl) and other drums with one skin, and for the *mattalam* and other drums with skin at both ends, and strings for *veenas* and *yaru* (a kind of *vīna* or South Indian guitar), and pigment (*gorochana*) for use in worship in the temples. He used to stand outside the entrance to temples, and with increasing love (*anbu*) would dance and sing (in honour of the deity). One day, when he was in Tiruppunkūr and was doing reverence to the god (*svāmi*), desirous of rendering holy homage he thought to himself "Oh that I could go and stand in the very entrance to the shrine, and see and do homage directly in the presence of the god!" Then the god, according to his desire, caused the image of the bull (*idapatevan*), which is placed as warden before the entrance to temples, and prevents profane glances from those who have no right to enter the shrine from falling on the god, to move to one side, and graciously gave sight of himself to his worshipper.

[This casual reference to the exclusion of Paraiyans from Saivite shrines points to the essential difference of cultus. The out-castes were not admitted to the shrines of Sīvan mentioned in this and other legends, because in origin they were the shrines of a higher, perhaps conquering race. On the other hand the lower cultus greatly influenced the higher, as a study of the modern forms of village *dēvata*-worship shows.]

o

Then Nandan, seeing a depression in the ground at that holy place, dug a tank for the temple, and went to his own village. In this way he went to many holy places, and did homage.

One day he felt a desire to go to Sithambaram, and by reason of the strength of that desire he could not sleep all that night. At dawn he mourned, saying "If I go to Sithambaram, my caste has no fitness to entitle me to enter the holy temple there."

[Sithambaram is one of the most holy, if not the holiest, of all Saiva shrines.]

Then he said "But even this is the grace of the god." Then he stayed where he was, but afterwards, by reason of the increase of his desire, he said "I will go on the holy day." Thus did he delay many days, saying "I will go on the holy day; I will go on the holy day;" and so he got the name "*Tirunāleipovār*" or "He will go on the holy day."

Then one day, being impelled by the desire to see Sithambaram, having set out from his own village, he reached the border of Sithambaram; and, having entered the gateway of the wall surrounding that town, he saw the sacred fire-sacrifice (*ōmam* Sankr. *hōma*) being made in the houses of the Brāhmans of the place. Then he was afraid to enter the place, and, having done reverence (*namaskāram*), he made a circuit of the boundary of the holy place.

[Tamil *valam* Sankr. *pradakshina* circumambulation of a temple or person, always keeping it or him to the right.]

Having done this night and day, considering the while on the impossibility of his entering (the holy precincts), Tirunāleipovār said to himself "How can I ever obtain sight of Sīva, the Lord of the Assembly (*i.e.*, of the holy ones in Sithambaram)? This degrading birth of mine (*i.e.*, the fact that I am a Paraiyan) is the hindrance, and so with sorrow he went to sleep. Then the Lord of the Assembly, willing to show grace to him and drive away his sorrow, appeared to him in a dream and graciously said to him "In order to avert the disgrace of thy birth thou must bathe in fire; having risen thou wilt come into our presence even along with Brāhmans." Then the god also appeared in a dream to the Holy Ones at Sithambaram, and commanded them to prepare the fire for Tirunāleipovār, and then disappeared.

The whole company of the Holy Ones at Sithambaram, when they awoke and arose and were assembled in the entrance to the shrine, said to each other "We will do according to the command of the Lord of the Assembly," and then they went to Tirunāleipovār and said "We have come to prepare fire for thee now by the command of the Lord of the Assembly." Having heard that, Tirunāleipovār said "I thy servant am blessed," and did reverence. Then the Brāhmans prepared the fire in a pit before the gate under the tower (*gōpuram*), outside the south wall, and announced it to Tirunāleipovār. Then he came to the place where the pit of fire was, and there he meditated in his mind on the holy feet of the Lord of the Assembly, and made a circuit round it, and worshipped, and entered it. Then this saint (*Nāyanār*) lost his old body, and obtained the form of a meritorious Brāhman sage, and arose wearing the sacred thread and his hair in the fashion of an ascetic. The Holy Ones of Sithambaram, and certain other Saivite devotees, saw this, and did reverence (*anjali*), being very joyful. Then Tirunāleipovār went in their company, approached the tower of the temple (*i.e.*, over the gateway), did reverence to it, rose up, entered the shrine, and reached the 'Golden Hall.' After that the Brāhmans and the rest of those who were there saw him no more, and marvelled much and praised (Sīvan). Thus the Lord of the Assembly allowed (Nandan the Pulaiyan called) Tirunāleipovār to approach his holy feet (lit. gave his holy feet to Tirunāleipovār).

A. C. CLAYTON.

SOME AGRICULTURAL CEREMONIES IN MALABAR.

The three great national festivals in Malabar are Ōnam, Vishu and Tiruvātira.

Of these, Vishu, the feast of the vernal equinox, is celebrated on the first of the Malabar month Mēdom between the 10th and 14th of April. To the Tamulians it is the New Year's day, but to the people of Malabar it marks the commencement of the new agricultural year. A Malabar agricultural proverb says "No hot weather after Vishu." The first thing seen on the morning of Vishu day is considered as an omen for the whole year. Every Malaiyāli takes care, therefore, to look on an auspicious object. Arrangements are accordingly made to have a kani, which means a sight or spectacle. In the preparation of this the following articles are absolutely necessary:—

Clean rice.
A clean newly-washed cloth.
A grandham (sacred book of cadjan).
Flowers of the konna tree (*Cassia Fistula*).
A cucumber.
A fruit called kōvaka (*Cephalandra indica*).
A cocoanut cut in two.
Mangoes.
Jāk fruit (*Artocarpus integrifolia*).
Gold jewelry.
Coins.
A bell-metal mirror (not glass).

On the evening before the festival, all these articles are arranged, in a particular order, inside a bell-metal vessel, which is covered with konna flowers. Oil is poured into the cocoanut cups, and lamp wicks are inserted therein. One of the members of the family sleeps close to the vessel, and gets up about two hours before dawn. A bell-metal lamp with five wicks, and the cocoanut lamps are then lighted, and the other members of the family called. Every one—man, woman and child—washes the hands, feet and face, smears sacred ashes over the body, and puts on new white cloths One by one the members of the family are brought in to have a look into the kani, and the elders may be heard warning those who are coming for the "first sight" to keep their eyes tightly closed. When near the kani, the subject is made to sit on a grass mat spread beside it, facing east. He is then told to hold the sides of the vessel, and look carefully at its contents. After the first sight, the elders make presents of money to the junior members of the family and the servants. Inauspicious objects for the first sight are similar to those ordinarily recognised as bad omens. To see, therefore, a single Brāhman, a woman with a broom-stick, a buffalo, etc., is believed to forebode ill-luck. Among animals, to see a jackal is considered very lucky; so much so that if a man has a run of good luck on a particular day, it is common to hear people exclaim "Was it a fox that he had as a first sight?" To see a cat, on the contrary, is considered unlucky.

After the distribution of money, the most important function on Vishu morning is the laying of the spade-furrow as a sign that cultivation operations have commenced. A spade, decorated with konna flowers, is brought, and a portion of the yard on the north side smeared with cow-dung and painted with powdered rice-water. An offering is made on the spot to Ganapathi (Ganēsa), and a member of the family, turning to the east, cuts the earth three times.

A ceremony on a grander scale is called the Chāl, which literally means a furrow, for an account of which we must begin with the visit of the astrologer (Kanisan) on Vishu eve. Every dēsam (hamlet) in Malabar has its own astrologer, who visits families under his jurisdiction on festive occasions. Accordingly, on the eve of the new agricultural year, every Hindu house in the district is visited by the Kanisans of the respective dēsams, who, for a modest present of rice, vegetables and oils, make a forecast of the season's prospects, which is engrossed on a cadjan (palm-leaf). This is called the Vishu phalam, which is obtained by comparing the nativity with the equinox. Special mention is made therein as to the probable rainfall from the position of the planets—highly-prized information in a district, where there are no irrigation works or large reservoirs for water. But the most important item in the forecast is the day and time at which the first ploughing is to take place. The chāl is one of the most impressive and solemn of the Malabar agricultural ceremonies, and, in its most orthodox form, is now prevalent only in the Palghāt tāluk. Other visitors on Vishu day are the carpenter with a plough, the blacksmith with a plough-share and a spade, and the basket-maker with a basket, to each of whom a present of rice; vegetables, and oils is made.

At the auspicious hour shown in the forecast, the master of the house, the cultivation agent and Cherumars (agrestic slaves) assemble in the barn. A portion of the yard in front of the building is painted with rice-water, and a lighted bell-metal lamp is placed near at hand with some paddy (unhusked rice) and rice, and several cups made of the leaves of the kanniram (*Strychnos Nux vomica*), as many cups as there are varieties of seed in the barn. Then, placing implicit faith in his gods and deceased ancestors, the master of the house opens the barn-door, followed by the Cheruman with a new painted basket containing the leaf cups. The master then takes a handful of seed from a seed-basket and fills one of the cups, and the cultivating agent, head Cheruman, and others who are interested in a good harvest, fill the cups till the seeds are exhausted. The basket, with the cups, is next taken to the decorated portion of the yard. A new plough-share is fastened to a new plough and a pair of cattle are brought on to the scene. Plough, cattle and basket are all painted with rice-water. A procession proceeds to the fields, on reaching which the head Cheruman lays down the basket, and makes a mound of earth with the spade. To this a little manure is added, and the master throws a handful of seed into it. The cattle are then yoked, and one turn is ploughed by the head Cheruman. Inside this at least seven furrows are made, and the plough is dropped to the right. An offering is made to Ganapathi, and the master throws some seed into a furrow. Next the head Cheruman calls out "May the gods on high and the deceased ancestors bless the seed which has been thrown broadcast, and the cattle which are let loose; the mother and children of the house, the master and the slaves. May they also vouchsafe to us a good crop, good sunshine, and a good harvest." A cocoanut is then cut on the plough-share, and from the cut portions several deductions are made. If the hinder portion is larger than the front one, it augurs an excellent harvest. If the nut is cut into two equal portions, the harvest will be moderate. If the cut passes through the eyes of the nut, or if no water is left in the cut portions, certain misfortune is foreboded. The cut fragments are then taken with a little water inside them, and a leaf of the tulsi plant (*Ocimum sanctum*) dropped in. If the leaf turns to the right, a prosperous harvest is assured;

whereas, if it turns to the left, certain calamity will follow. This ceremonial concluded, there is much shouting, and the names of all the gods may be heard called out in a confused prayer. The party then breaks up, and the unused seeds are divided among the workmen.

The actual sowing of the seed takes place towards the middle of May. The local deity who is responsible for good crops is Cherukunnath Bhagavathi, who is also called Annapūrana, and is worshipped in the Chirakkal taluk. Before the seed is sown, a small quantity, according to the capacity of the family, is set apart as an offering to the goddess Annapūrna Īswari. By July the crops should be ready for harvesting, and the previous year's stock is running low. Accordingly, several ceremonies are crowded into the month Karkitakam (July-August). When the sun passes from the sign of Gemini to Cancer, *i.e.*, on the last day of Mithuna (June-July), a ceremony called the driving away of Potti (evil spirit) is performed in the evening. The house is cleaned, and the rubbish collected in an old winnowing basket. A woman rubs oil on her head, and, taking the basket, goes three times round the house, while children run after her, calling out Potti, phoo (run away, evil spirit). On the following morning the good spirit is invoked, and asked to bless every householder and give a good harvest. Before dawn a handful of veli, a wild yam (*Caladium nymphaeiflorum*) and turmeric, together with ten herbs called dasapushpam (= ten flowers), such as are worn in the head by Nambūtiri Brāhman ladies after the morning bath, are brought in. They are—

(1) Nilappana (*Curculigo orchioides*).
(2) Karuka (*Cynodon Dactylon*).
(3) Cherupoola (*Ærua lanata*).
(4) Muyalchevi (*Emelia sonchifolia*).
(5) Puvamkurunthala (*Vernonia cinerea*).
(6) Ulinuà (*Cardiospermum Halicacabum*).
(7) Mukutti (*Biophytum sensitivum*).
(8) Thiruthāli (*Ipomœa sepiaria*).
(9) Kannunni (*Eclipta alba*).
(10) Krishnakananthi (*Evolvulus alsinoides*).

Each of the above is believed to be the special favourite of some god or goddess, *e.g.*, Nilappana of the god of riches, Thiruthāli of the wife of Kāma, the god of love, etc. They are stuck in the front eaves of every house with some cow-dung. Then, before daybreak, Sri Bhagavathi is formally installed, and her symbolical presence is continued daily til the end of the month Karkitagam. A plank, such as is used by Malaiyālis when they sit at meals, is well washed and smeared with ashes. On it are placed a mirror, a potful of ointment made of sandal, camphor, musk and saffron, a small round box containing red paint, a goblet full of water, and a grāndham (sacred book of cadjan), usually Dēvi-Mahāthmyam, *i.e.*, song in praise of Bhagavathi. By its side the ten flowers are set. On the first day of Karkitagam in some places, an attempt is made to convert the malignant Kāli into a beneficent deity. From Calicut northward this ceremonial is celebrated, for the most part by children, on a grand scale. From early morning they may be seen collecting ribs of plantain leaves, with which they make representations of a ladder, cattle-shed, plough and yoke. Representations of cattle are made from the leaves of the jāk tree (*Artocarpus integrifolia*). These are placed in an old winnowing basket. The materials for a feast are placed in a pot, and the toy agricultural articles and the pot are carried round each house simultaneously three times, while the children call out "Kalia, Kalia, Monster, Monster, receive our offering and give us plenty of seed and wages, protect our cattle and bulls, and support our fences." The various articles are then placed under a jāk tree, on the eastern side of the house if possible.

The next important ceremony is called the Nira, or the bringing in of the first-fruits. It is celebrated about the middle of Karkitagam. The house is cleaned, and the doors and windows are cleansed with the rough leaves of a tree called pārakam (*Ficus hispida*) and decorated with white rice-paint. The walls are whitewashed, and the yard is smeared with cow-dung. The ten flowers (desapushpam) are brought to the gate of the house, together with leaves, etc., of the following :—

Athi (*Ficus glomerata*).
Ithi (*Ficus infectoria*).
Arayāl (*Ficus religiosa*).
Péral (*Ficus bengalensis*).
Illi (Bamboo tender leaves).
Nelli (*Phyllanthus Emblica*).
Jāk (*Artocarpus integrifolia*).
Mango (*Mangifera indica*).

On the morning of the ceremony, the priest of the local temple comes out therefrom, preceded by a man blowing a conch shell. This is a signal for the whole village, and every householder sends out a male member, duly purified by a bath and copiously smeared with sacred ashes, to the fields to gather some ears of paddy. Sometimes the paddy for the nira is brought from the temple, instead of the field. It is not necessary to pluck the paddy from one's own fields. Free permission is given to gather it from any field in which it may be ripe. When the paddy is brought near the house, the above said leaves are taken out from the gate-house, where they had been kept overnight, and the ears of paddy laid thereon. The bearer thereof is met at the gate by a woman of the house with a lighted lamp. The new paddy is then carried to the house in procession, those assembled crying out: "Fill, fill; increase, increase; fill the house; fill the baskets; fill the stomachs of the children." In a portion of the verandah, which is decorated with rice-paint, a small plank, with a plantain leaf on it, is set. Round this the man who bears the paddy goes three times, and, turning due east, places the burden on the leaf. On the right is set the lighted lamp. An offering of cocoanuts and sweets is made to Ganapathi, and the above said leaves and ears of paddy are attached to various parts of the house, the agricultural implements, and even to trees. A sumptuous repast brings the ceremony to a close. At Palghāt, when the new paddy is carried in procession, the people say: "Fill like the Kottāram in Kozhalmannam; fill like the expansive sands of the Pērār." Now this Kottāram is eight miles west of Palghāt. According to Dr. Gundert, the word means a store-house or a place where temple affairs are managed. It is a ruined building with crumbling walls, lined inside with laterite, and outside with slabs of granite. It was the granary of the Maruthūr temple adjoining it. The story goes that the supply in this granary was inexhaustible.

The next ceremony of importance is called Puthari (meal of new rice). In some places it takes place on nira day, but, as a rule, it is an independent festival, which takes place before the great national festival, Onam, in August. When the new rice crop has been threshed, a day is fixed for puthari. Those who have no cultivation simply add some grains of the new rice to their meal. An indispensible curry on this day is made of the leaves of *Cassia Tora*, peas, the fruit of puthari chundanga (*Swertia Chirata*) brinjals (*Solanum Melongena*) and green pumpkins. The first crop is now harvested. There are no special ceremonies connected with the cultivation of the second crop, except the one called Chĕttotakam in the month of Thulam (November) which is observed in the Palghāt taluk. It is an offering made to the gods, when the transplantation is completed, to wipe out the sins the labourers may have committed by unwittingly killing the insects and reptiles concealed in the earth. The god, whose protection is invoked on this occasion, is called Muni. No barn is complete without its own Muni, who is generally represented by a block of granite beneath a tree. He is the protector of cattle and field labourers, and arrack, toddy, and blood form necessary ingredients for his worship. In well-to-do families a goat is sacrificed to him, but the poorer classes satisfy him with the blood of a fowl. The officiating priest is generally the cultivation agent of the family, who is a Nāyar, or sometimes a Cheruman. The goat or fowl is brought before the god, and a mixture of turmeric and chunām sprinkled over it. If the goat or fowl shakes, it is a sign that the god is satisfied. If it does not, the difficulty is got over by a very liberal interpretation of the smallest movement of the animal, and a further application of the mixture. The god who ensures sunshine and good weather is Mullan. He is a rural deity, and is set up on the borders or ridges of the rice fields. Like Muni, he is confined to the Palghāt taluk, and is propitiated by the sacrifice of a fowl. Other deities responsible for the weal or woe of the cattle are Mundian and Parakutti. The former is an incarnation or sakti of Sīva, and is worshipped in the good or bad form with or without arrack, toddy and blood. When a cow has calved, pollution is observed for ten days. She is milked only on the eleventh day. The whole of the milk drawn on that day is boiled with rice, and made with sugar into a payasam, which is offered to Mundian in the good form, or with arrack, toddy and the sacrifice of a fowl in the bad form. The offering is made by a member or even servant of the family in the night, and, when the pūja is over, all retire, leaving the spot free for Mundian to come and partake of the offering. Parakutti is a malignant deity, and he is, as the name signifies, the Paraiyan god. Blood, arrack and toddy are absolutely necessary in his worship.

The second crop is harvested in Makaram (end of January), and a festival, called Uchāral (corresponding to the Februations of the Romans) is observed from the twenty-eighth to the thirtieth in honour of the menstruation of mother earth, which is believed to take place on those days, which are observed as day of abstinence from all work, except hunting. The first day is called the closing of Uchāral. Towards evening some thorns, five or six broom-sticks, and ashes are taken to the room where the grain is stored. The door is closed, and the thorns and sticks are placed against it, or fixed to it with cow-dung. The ashes are spread before it, and during that and the following day no one will open the door. A complete holiday is also given to the Cherumans. On the second day cessation from work is scrupulously observed. The house may not be cleaned, and the daily smearing of the floor with cow-dung is avoided. Even gardens may not be watered. On the fourth day the Uchāral is opened, and a basketful of dry leaves is taken to the fields, and burnt with a little manure. The Uchāra days are the quarter days of Malabar, and demands for surrender of property may be made only on the day following the festival, when all agricultural leases expire. By the burning of leaves and manure on his estate, the cultivator, it seems to me, proclaims to the world that he remains in possession of the property. In support of this view, we have the practice of a new lessee asking the lessor whether any other person has burnt dry leaves in the field. By a liberal interpretation of the term "the day after the Uchāral," the Courts have extended the period of demand up to the Vishu, *i.e.*, the day of the vernal equinox. The Uchāral festival is also held at Cherupulcherri, and at Kanayam near Shoranur. Large crowds assemble with representations of cattle in straw, which are taken in procession to the temple of Bagavathi with the usual beating of drums and the shouting of the crowd.

No books have been consulted in the preparation of this paper, and no ceremony has been described, which has not actually been seen by me.

C. KARUNAKARA MENON, B.A.